KS LEGACY

14 Points Of Kevin Samuels
All High Value Black Men Must Know

Lionel Davids

Invierno Viniendo Publishing

© 2022 Lionel Davids

Invierno Viniendo Publishing

All Rights Reserved.

Lioneldavids.substack.com

ISBN: 978-1-387-90468-6

CONTENTS

Chapter	Title	Page
	Dedication	5
1	The Value of Inherent Value For Black Men	6
2	14 Points All High Value Black Men Must Know	10
3	Show Your Work, Get What You Are Worth & Be Excellent	18
	Suggested Books	20
	Suggested Documentaries, Movies & Websites	24
	Suggested YouTube & Patreon Channels	26

Thanks to all of you who believe in fighting for faith in God, traditional nuclear familes, open opportunities for the success of men and women and the rights and obligations of all countries to protect these.

DEDICATION

Dedicated to the great Kevin Samuels.

Thank you brother for your commitment, your work, your advice, your laughter and your words of warning to help make us all better men and women.

Thank You Almighty God for this brother whom those who love and appreciate his service affectionately call "the godfather".

May You, Most High God, Be Pleased with his good work among us, forgive our brother's shortcomings and accept him into your Eternal Presence.

In Jesus' (Yoshua's) Name,

Amen.

CHAPTER ONE

THE VALUE OF INHERENT VALUE FOR BLACKMEN

Black men and indeed all men have an inherent value that is not subservient to nor assigned by the women in their lives or outside of their lives. This innate value is also not assigned by other men. Indeed it is God Given.

Too many Black women and Black men (as well as many others) have been influenced, trained and even commanded by Feminism and Feminist ideals to get men to:

A. Constantly chase women and their issues verbally, psychologically, financially and physically. He is expected to constantly "kiss her backside" for access to her. He can be almost endlessly strung along to do her bidding for the mere possibility of sex if he allows this game to be run on him.

B. Only value himself by what he has done in service to her most recently. "Whatcha' gonna' do for me?" easily becomes "What have you done for me lately?" with calculated reservation.

C. Chase her again constantly on reset by keeping difficult issues at the forefront of the relationship or marriage, playing the mad and difficult role or the sad and indifferent one.

Playing the sighing victim is a large part of this.

D. Waste his resources on her by spoiling her with gifts, paying her bills, giving her money and constantly keeping her buffered from accountability, consequences and responsibility.

E. Consistently testing his patience and measuring how much pain, difficulty, inconvenience and even death he is willing to endure or chance on her behalf.

All of these things cloud a man's judgement, takes away time from his God Given purpose, increases stress and gets on his nerves. No man who knows himself and has self respect tolerates any of this and quickly gets her out of his life or removes himself from the situation.

High Value Men (HVM) exist among all ethnic groups everywhere. Every one of them have a moral value made and measured by themselves, higher financial value and higher intrinsic value. They have certain characteristics that they share that make them "High Value" as men including:

A. They are single but with options to date who they choose.

B. They have singularity of purpose by focusing on their purpose first and foremost. This purpose in 3-5 years should generate a 6-7 figure annual income for them or higher.

C. They demand respect and are confident and this is exemplified in how they dress and by carrying themselves with sagacity and class.

D. They deal predominantly with a network of like-minded men.

E. They are proudly and happily masculine and want "Fit, Feminine and Friendly" (FFF) women who are stylish, classy, intelligent, have excellent homemaking skills and have some kind of artistic sensibility or ability.

Anyone that willfully or subconsciously seeks to prevent a man from being or becoming a High Value Man needs to be ostracized, locked up or should be in therapy.

Therapy should be therapeutic and does not necessarily come from modern religious institutions that are strongly influenced by Feminist women and men. Many (not all) preachers, rabbis, imams, priests and ministers find it difficult to speak in favour of masculine men and feminine women for fear of losing revenue from their congregations. Too many also have problems resisting the wives of men they are supposedly helping and also the women themselves who may seek them for counsel. Some have difficulty resisting those of the same sex they are "counselling" as well as contributing to the corruption of small children.

Therapy should be sought from professional therapists, psychiatrists and psychologists with accompanying elders and teachers. The ultimate goal of therapy should be to heal, have the ability to handle reality better, become more helpful to one's self and others and improve one's overall appearance value.

Improving appearance value and self worth should include daily work on the following areas:

A. Improving how you dress as a man or a woman.

Men should have solid, business color (black, dark blue, grey, brown) suits. Women should have solid, business colored dresses and business suits. There should be at least one day out of every week that adults dress this way no matter if they are white collar or blue collar.

B. Attitude and behaviour. Disrespect should be minimalized at all costs. Unjust critics should be ignored as much as humanly possible.

C. Improve your affiliations and associations. Get people out of your life that are not supportive of your purpose, personality and being. Surround yourself with a team of like-minded individuals.

D. Make better life choices by staying away from people who consistently make bad ones. There is no rehabilitating the foolish. You will only end up wasting your time, being used and losing much in the way of resources and time.

E. Take care of your weight and health. Achieve and maintain a healthy athletic weight, eat healthily and see a doctor on a regular basis.

In conclusion, any man or concerned woman that works on improving themselves according to the above mentioned points will find themselves on the road to self improvement, success and High Value.

CHAPTER TWO

14 POINTS ALL HIGH VALUE BLACK MEN MUST KNOW

1. High Value Black men have options and exercise options in dating freely and without recourse.

They do this simply because they can. They do not allow themselves to be restricted by religious dogma nor secular philosophy or secular ethics. They have become Kings, so to speak, in their own right by their own ingenuity, hard work, creativity, discipline, perserverance and endurance. They live as a law unto themselves without breaking the de juris law of the land in which they live or do business. They are not required to fully commit to any one woman. They require dedication from all that they deal with closely.

The most powerful men of history have lived in this manner including Kings David and Solomon, Augustus Caesar, Genghis Khan, Louis XIV and Shaka Zulu.

Musicians, pro athletes, moguls, CEOs and other men at the top of their fields exercise these options at will.

2. Average at best men have little to no options other than average at best women or less.

These men can exercise no other option without difficult consequences (ie: being labeled a "cheater", break ups, getting "cheated" on in return, divorce etc.....). They may be able to date or sleep with High Value Women but they lack the ability to exercise other options while being with her. She is the de facto leader and he will invariably and unmistakenly be the follower until she tires of him and dismisses him.

3. All Black women want what they perceive to be a High Value Black man.

In her elementary years that may be the boy she finds "cute", funny or the rare boy that will actually play house with her. In her teen years that young man is the strongest, smartest or most attractive. He may also be the one with the nicest clothes, money or a car/truck. The most desired at this point are athletes, musicians, the best dancers, the toughest fighters, the wild and unruly, the most physically attractive, thugs, criminals and those with displayed leadership ability.

There is little to no deviation from this as they age. What they say they want is not what they seek after or sleep with. They oftentimes repeat what is popular or expected as they age and by their mid 40s to mid 50s they realize their sexual market value has declined exceedingly in comparison to women in their late teens to early 30s. All religious, social, political, psychological, cosmetic, romantic, familial and financial activity they engage in is because of or in response to their perceived value and their ability or inability to be selected by a Black HVM.

4. All Black women do not want what they perceive to be an average at best or below man.

They do not like settling. Whatever the society, general media, social media, their friends or her female competitors consider High Value that is generally what she desires or seeks after. This is summarized in the saying "The Alpha male fucks, the

Beta male bucks." She will settle for the beta for reputation, comfort, bills and reliability but her secret and real desire and leaning will be towards the men she perceives as dominant. The previous point three described how this changes as they get older and is directly related to the inevitable realization that menopause is a purely female experience, men do not have a biological clock, and that older men generally have more experience, are more mechanically inclined and are more settled in their being with more resources. She may simply choose to settle while sleeping with what she perceives as the Alpha or HVM on the side if the Alpha or HVM does not engage her with any degree of seriousness.

5. High Value Black Men and HV men in general do not like morbidly obese women (Big Shirleys).

It's more than just a matter of expanded visual symmetry or the lack thereof altogether because she is just too big.

To HV men and men in general, morbidly obese women represent two things:

A. Poor self image.

B. A lack of discipline with healthy food choices and exercise.

These two drive the following conclusion:

Her lack of discipline will also be reflected in her sexual activity, choices and lack of being selective. Many will say "Oh, I've been with a HVM" (sexually). However, most cannot say there were any prospects for a real relationship or marriage.

A HVM perceives her "Big Shirleyness" as temporary fun, a "roll in the hay", a one night stand or an "old reliable" at best if she is "cute" or considered "big but pretty". He sees a higher grocery bill, unnecessary health issues and general laziness.

6. Women with multiple children by multiple men are generally taboo for all HV men.

This is not Sade's "Sweetest Taboo".

It is considered to be a bad business decision as he can be attached to child support issues and end up paying for a legacy that is not his own. The common denominator in her failed relationships is her or her poor choices. Lastly, it doesn't look good for him visually before his business associates and family. A HVM generally sees this as little more than trouble and a bad look and even an occasional night of pleasure isn't worth the effort or potential risk in the "Post Me Too Era."

7. Too many Black women are generally unrealistic & delusional about their own sexual market value.

Too many are confused about what they can physically attract for temporary pleasure and what they can actually hold for long term relationships and/or marriage.

They base their aspirations on what Coach Greg Adams refers to as "The Hope Strategy". They believe they can or will acquire a HVM by religious misinterpretation ("Jesus will send me a man."), mind manipulation, sex, fake femininity and an envious overadmiration for and competiton with the very few women who may have "hit the lotto" and are married to a HVM.
"Ciara's Prayer" becomes their mantra for the slim possibility of making that buzzer beater shot with little time on the biological clock.

8. There a 5-7 times more High Value Women than there are High Value Men of all ethnic groups combined.

The "average at best" woman generally cannot compete with these women for anything lasting or serious.

She literally has little to no chance.

9. Too many Black women see Black men in general as commodities in a chattel slavery way.

They perceive them as sexual studs and monetary resources (a dick and a wallet) when they like them or find them attractive and view them as villains, pariahs and are indifferent, inhumane, disrespectful and hostile towards them when they are not interested.

10. Too many Black men, in the western world especially, have been reprogrammed to dislike self improvement.

Too many brothers in the U.S., Canada, The U.K., Australia etc, have been bamboozled into accepting hopelessness, social rejection and a lack of ambition as "Reality" or "Keeping it Real".

This is exemplified through:

A. A lack of interest in reading books, watching documentaries, or listening to any music that is not criminalized Hip Hop that accepts or celebrates the street life as the only possibility for Black men even in the face of countless historical and current examples to the contrary from Benjamin Banneker and Garrett Morgan to Bob Marley and Ben Carson.

B. A lack of interest in Men's Fashion ie: Properly fitting suits, ties, black socks, dress shoes, wallets, leather or snakeskin belts, button shirts with collars, work boots, ironed pants, leather jackets of a solid color, trench coats and hats (not baseball caps). This is coupled with an incessant refusal to divorce hoodies, tennis shoes when not playing ball or working out and sexually psychologically questionable "sagging" which strangely doesn't go the way of most styles and simply play out.

C. A lack of interest in being both spiritual and legally assertive economically.

E. A self regenerating inability to overcome envying the success, looks, confidence, style or sexual market value of another Black man.

11. The majority of Black women who disagree with points 1-9 are strongly influenced by social media, screen writers, program directors, college professors, politicians, song writers and "Reality TV" persons that are Feminist influenced. They rarely if ever see or interact critically with any of these people and simply believe what they present, teach, say or show without questioning any of it.

They are generally unread, unstudied, obese (Big Shirley), financially lacking or bankrupt, have serious psychological, moral, spiritual, intellectual, grammatical and ethical challenges that they are unwilling to deal with. Many do not realize they probably need professional therapy immediately.

Most of these disageeable ones are also too old for anything serious (Leftover Women, Sheng Nu in China, Old Maids or Spinsters in the West), too difficult to get along with (even with other women), too tiring to deal with in terms of always being either mad or sad, lacking in physical attraction to a broad range of men (like most Black women Feminists) and lacking in the ability to look at "The Woman In The Mirror" for accountability and responsibility for their own life choices.

They are hopelessly trapped in a cycle of defaulting to the use of SIGN Language (Shame, Insults, Guilt and the Need to be "right") when faced with spiritual, historic, statistical, intrinsic and biological truth.

12. The majority of Black men who disagree with 1-10 or 1-11 are too financially lacking (broke) or too financially inept to be taken seriously for relationships or marriages with FFF women or HV women. These men are also generally obese or out of shape, too undisciplined, too anti social, too unattractive, too lazy and too envious to work effectively with other Black men in a specialized way to achieve goals bigger than the individual self.

They also use SIGN Language because they been primarily miseducated, trained and influenced by far less than average at best women and/or men who are afraid to deviate from the standard low accomplishment talking points and agenda.

13. Stop dumbing yourself down to impress.

Do not play the fool in front of supposedly "cool" people just to fit in. If they discourage you from being good or excellent then you don't need them nor do you need to be around them. Don't be concerned if they refer to you as "arrogant". This is an indication that they don't have what it takes to compete and want you to settle for less from yourself and for yourself.

Find new friends that value intelligence, style and excellence.

14. Ignore your haters and unjust critics and keep pushing forward.

Listen to constructive criticism from your team or closest associates that are trustworthy, upstanding men.

Tell all others who make personal, verbal or media attacks to "go kick rocks" in your mind.

Stay focused on your spirit, purpose, health and wealth.

CHAPTER THREE

SHOW YOUR WORK, GET WHAT YOU ARE WORTH

&

BE EXCELLENT

Men should be CIA (Confident, Intelligent and Assertive).

Ladies should be FBI (Feminine, Beautiful and Intelligent).

Be the best you can be everyday. Don't half step or slack off. Don't cheat time. Use time wisely and always build and offer a better product. Take time to properly rest, nourish, recharge, plan and begin again. Excellence is your God Given birthright. Go for it everyday.

Life is about relationships.

Real relationships are about reaching out, communicating, listening, giving encouraging advice, using your leverage and skill to build and expand beyond that block, neighborhood, city, state or country you grew up in.

Men, brothers, stop dressing like "shit". Dress like a man.

Have a dress up business or church day at least once a week. Improve your image and have a look of success to draw success.

Work hard, work smart, enjoy life, eat and drink healthily, consult your doctor periodically, touch bases with your team, relax, rest and repeat.

Build a culture of success.

Build a team of 5 men with different skill sets to transition the idea of improving Black men's image aggressively and immediately. Improve Black men's image by bringing new and improved visual images in media, movies, education, business and music.

It's time for Black men's media networks.

Start them. Own them. Control them. Never sell them. Nothing beats productivity for yourself.

Black men everywhere we need our own:

1. Social Media Video Platforms similar to Patreon or YouTube.

2. Version of Amazon or Barnes & Noble Online.

3. Gaming Production Companies

4. Record Companies and Distribution Focusing On Jazz, Reggae, Funk and African Music.

5. IT Techs (More)

6. Photographers and Filmmakers

7. Program Directors

8. Film Crews

9. Armed Security Companies

10. Young Black Men's Mechanics & Media Bootcamps.

11. Young Black Men's Literacy, Bible Study, & Science Bootcamps.

12. Young Black Men's Business, Medicine and Martial Arts Bootcamps.

Find the productive things that you love and DO THEM!

SUGGESTED BOOKS

1. *The Book of Obsidian* — Mumia Obsidian Ali
2. *Subverted* — Sue Ellen Browder
3. *Shaka Zulu* — EA Ritter
4. *The Fall of America* — Elijah Muhammad
5. *What Color Is Your God?* — Colombus Salley
6. *The Kebra Negast* — Miguel F. Brooks
7. *The Original African Heritage Bible* — Cain Hope Felder
8. *Entreprenuership For Dummies* — Kathleen Allen
9. *World's Great Men of Color* — JA Rogers
10. *The Soul of Black Folk* — WEB DuBois
11. *The Blackman's Guide to Understanding The Blackwoman* — Shahrazad Ali
12. *The Blackwoman's Guide to Understanding The Blackman* — Shahrazad Ali
13. *The Feminist Mistake* — Mary A. Kassian
14. *The Manipulated Man* — Ester Vilar

15. *Madrigal's Magic Key to Spanish*

          Margarita Madrigal

16. *Learning Mandarin Chinese Characters*

          Yi Ren

17. *The Rational Male*   Rollo Tomassi

18. *Dressing The Man*   Alan Flusser

19. *Details Men's Style Manual*

          Daniel Peres

20. *The Emperor of Scent*   Chandler Burr

21. *A Natural History of The Senses*

          Diane Ackerman

22. *They Were Her Property*   Stephanie E. Jones Rogers

23. *Winter Is Coming*   Carolyne Larrington

24. *The Beginner's Guide to Engineering*

          Mark Huber

25. *Personal Image Enhancement*

          Dwayne A. George

26. *The Black Family Reunion Cookbook*

          The National Council of Negro Women

27. *The Endangered Black Family*

          Dr. Nathan Hare

28. *The Free Agent Lifestyle*   Coach Greg Adams

29. *Countering The Conspiracy to Destroy Black Boys*

    Dr. Jawanza Kunjufu

30. *Legend of The Streetfighter*

    Andre Joseph

31. *The U.S. Child Support System & The Black Family*

    DeMico Boothe

32. *Affirmations For Black Men*

    Willie Brown

33. *African Holistic Health*   Dr. Llaila O. Afrika

34. *CPR & First Aid Training Manual*

    EMS Safety Services Inc.

35. *The Black Manosphere Magazine*

    Dr. Spencer Holman

36. *Alpha Money Strategies*   Alpha Male Strategies

37. *God, The Blackman & Truth*

    Rabbee Ben Ammi

38. *SAS Survival Handbook*   John Lofty Wiseman

39. *The Man's No Nonsense Guide to Women*

    Marc H. Rudov

40. *The 48 Laws of Power*   Robert Greene

41. *It's Bigger Than Hip Hop*   M.K. Asante Jr.

42. *Up From Slavery* — Booker T. Washington

43. *The Philosophy & Opinions of Marcus Garvey* — Amy Jacques Garvey

44. *The Autobiography of Malcolm X as Told to Alex Haley* — Alex Haley, Malcolm X

45. *How to Win Friends & Influence People* — Dale Carnegie

46. *Powernomics* — Dr. Claud Anderson

47. *Workout War by Men's Health Magazine* — Jim Cotta

48. *The Power of Positive Thinking* — Norman Vincent Peale

49. *The Miseducation of The Negro* — Dr. Carter G. Woodson

50. *The Isis Papers* — Dr. Frances Cress Welsing

51. *From Babylon to Timbuktu* — Dr. Rudolph Windsor

52. *Dallas and The Jack Ruby Trial: Memoir of Judge Joe Brown Sr.* — Judge Joe Brown Sr.

SUGGESTED DOCUMENTARIES, MOVIES & WEBSITES

1. The Red Pill (Documentary starring Cassie Jaye)
2. Roots (TV Miniseries)
3. Roots: The Next Generation
4. Eyes On The Prize (Documentary Series)
5. The Vanishing Family: Crisis In Black America (Bill Moyers 1986 Special)
6. Blackdemographics.com
7. Game of Thrones Complete Series
8. The Matrix
9. The Walking Dead Complete Series
10. Rosewood
11. BabyBoy
12. The Tuskegee Airmen
13. Rebel Music: The Bob Marley Story
14. Purple Rain
15. Star Wars
16. Star Wars: The Empire Strikes Back

17. Star Wars: Return of The Jedi

18. Diary of a Tired Black Man

19. Boomerang

20. Color of The Cross

21. Higher Learning

22. The Hurricane

23. Mo' Better Blues

24. The Godfather 1-3

25. Lean On Me

26. From Hebrews to Negroes (Documentary)

27. Casino

28. Rich Dad's Guide to Wealth (Robert Kiyosaki)

29. Trading Places

30. The Wolf of Wall Street

31. The Art of War

32. The Art of War 2

SUGGESTED YOUTUBE & PATREON CHANNELS

1. Kevin Samuels
2. BlackRam313
3. Dennis Spurling
4. O'Shay Duke Jackson
5. The Lead Attorney
6. The Obsidian Media Network
7. The Crimson Cure
8. Rivah TV
9. Kiesha Arielle
10. DeeDee
11. Chantelle Simone
12. BGS IBMOR
13. Anton Daniels
14. The Kosher Clinician
15. Mediocre Tutorials & Reviews
16. Redd Blackscorpion
17. Manosphere Highlights Daily
18. Jaye De Black

19. Master Song Kung Fu

20. Damien Patrick

21. Get Licensed Security Insider

22. Dr. T. Hasan Johnson

23. Sandman

24. Stephiscold

25. Book of Alpharonomy

26. Melanie King

27. Dr. Michelle Daf

28. Rational Male Clips

29. The Style O.G.

30. Mr. Palmer

Mr. Kevin Samuels

© 2022 Lionel Davids

Invierno Viniendo Publishing

Lioneldavids.substack.com

ISBN: 978-1-387-90468-6

Lightning Source UK Ltd.
Milton Keynes UK
UKHW022322080223
416728UK00007B/83